NEFERTITI

"The heiress, great in favor, lady of grace, sweet of love, mistress of South and North, fair of face, happy with the two plumes, beloved of the living Aten, the chief wife of the King whom he loves, lady of the Two Lands, great of love, Nefertiti, living for ever and ever."

She wears the sun disk of the Aten and the feathers of Ma'at, goddess of Truth, and offers a bouquet to the Aten. Her daughter is clanging a sistrum.

Nefertiti, early period, c. year 8, from a column fragment now in the Ashmolean Museum, Oxford

Queen Nefertiti reigned until about Year 12 of King Akhenaten's reign, 1379 to 1362 B.C. Many of the following pictures are after drawings made from damaged reliefs and paintings found in the tombs of important functionaries of the day by N. de G. Davies for the Egypt Exploration Fund.

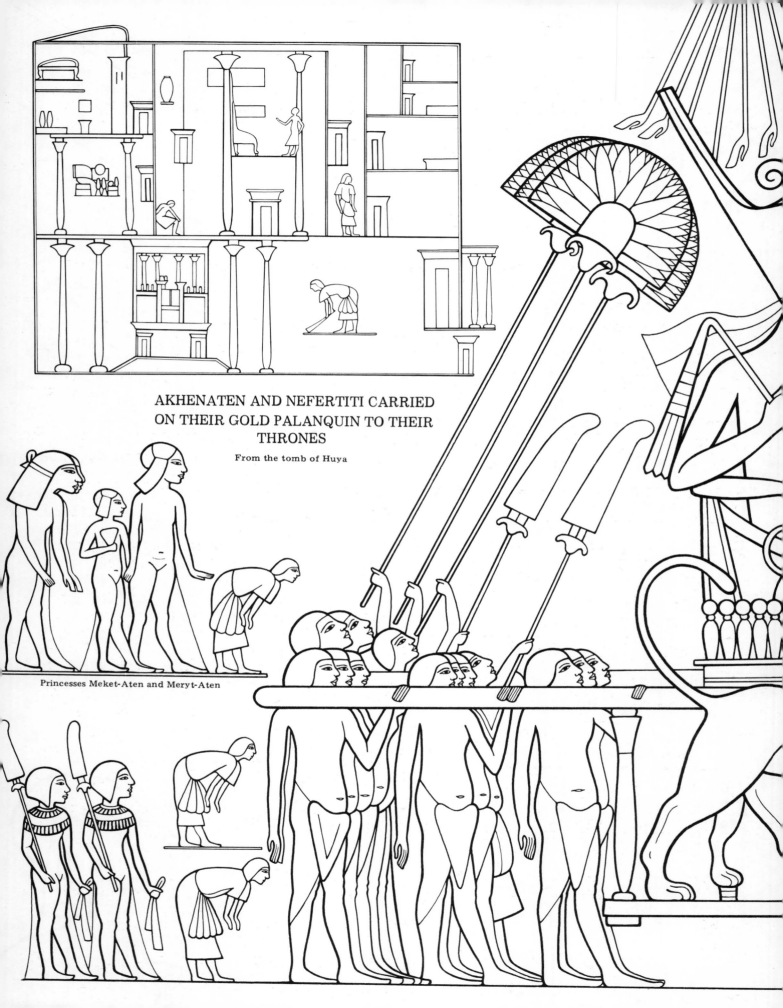

AKHENATEN AND NEFERTITI CARRIED
ON THEIR GOLD PALANQUIN TO THEIR
THRONES

From the tomb of Huya

Princesses Meket-Aten and Meryt-Aten

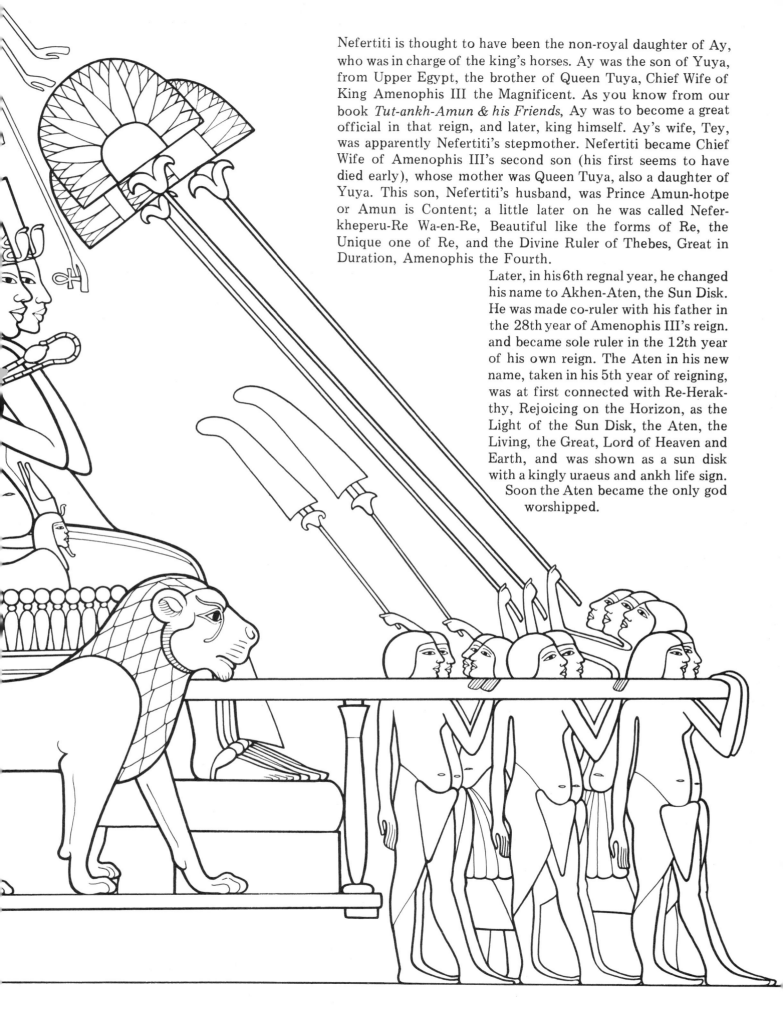

Nefertiti is thought to have been the non-royal daughter of Ay, who was in charge of the king's horses. Ay was the son of Yuya, from Upper Egypt, the brother of Queen Tuya, Chief Wife of King Amenophis III the Magnificent. As you know from our book *Tut-ankh-Amun & his Friends*, Ay was to become a great official in that reign, and later, king himself. Ay's wife, Tey, was apparently Nefertiti's stepmother. Nefertiti became Chief Wife of Amenophis III's second son (his first seems to have died early), whose mother was Queen Tuya, also a daughter of Yuya. This son, Nefertiti's husband, was Prince Amun-hotpe or Amun is Content; a little later on he was called Nefer-kheperu-Re Wa-en-Re, Beautiful like the forms of Re, the Unique one of Re, and the Divine Ruler of Thebes, Great in Duration, Amenophis the Fourth.

Later, in his 6th regnal year, he changed his name to Akhen-Aten, the Sun Disk. He was made co-ruler with his father in the 28th year of Amenophis III's reign. and became sole ruler in the 12th year of his own reign. The Aten in his new name, taken in his 5th year of reigning, was at first connected with Re-Herak-thy, Rejoicing on the Horizon, as the Light of the Sun Disk, the Aten, the Living, the Great, Lord of Heaven and Earth, and was shown as a sun disk with a kingly uraeus and ankh life sign. Soon the Aten became the only god worshipped.

THE SIX DAUGHTERS

Ankhes-en-pa-Aten, Meket-Aten, Meryt-Aten

Sotpe-en-Re, Nefer-neferu-Re, Nefer-neferu-Aten

THE KING AND QUEEN ENTHRONED

Year 12, from the tomb of Mery-Re

When Akhen-aten took this name, Nefertiti took the name Nefer-neferu-Aten, Fair is the Goddess of the Aten. Thebes had been the city of the old god Amun; its name was changed to Radiance of the Aten, at Tell el Amarna, midway between Thebes and Memphis. The tombs of the great officials of that era were made there and were covered with truly gorgeous scenes of Akhenaten and Nefer-titi and their daughters. Akhenaten is shown most often wearing the Blue Crown , or war helmet, as he was descended from the fighting kings of the 18th Dynasty who had chased the Hyksos out of Egypt and who conquered the peoples of Asia and Nubia. Nefertiti also wore a blue hat which matched the king's. A sphinx wore one like it, and it may have symbolized Queen Nefertiti as a sun goddess.

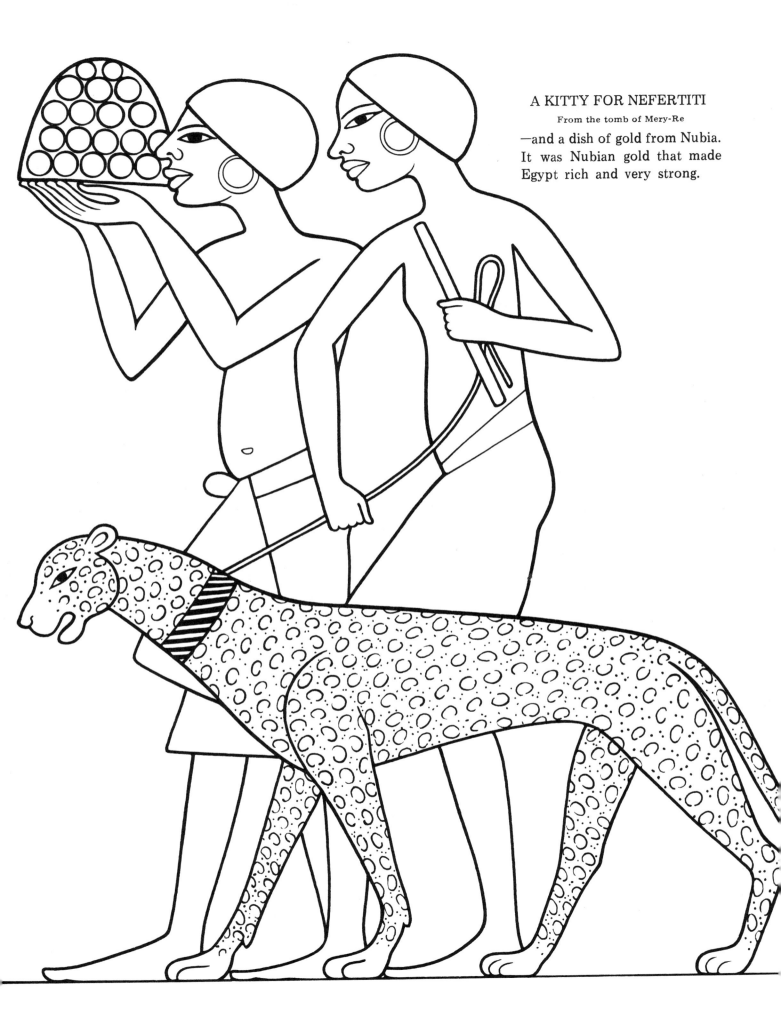

A KITTY FOR NEFERTITI

From the tomb of Mery-Re

—and a dish of gold from Nubia.
It was Nubian gold that made
Egypt rich and very strong.

THE WINDOW of APPEARANCES

The king and queen are looking out to see Parennefer the Craftsman of the king, rewarded. The Aten's rays keep the king and queen from falling out the window.

From the tomb of Parennefer

"O Pharoah, millions of years and myriads of festivals, the bright child of the Aten, who has afforded a sight of thyself to us. Thou sparklest with the brightness of the living Atten. Thou seest his beautiful rays mulitplying for the tale of festivals. He hath transferred to thee every land. . . " —Parennefer

THE HAPPY FAMILY

From a fragment from Amarna
now in the Musée du Louvre

From the tomb of Apy

OFFERING TO THE ATEN

The king and queen are offering containers of unguent with cartouches of the Aten at altars loaded with meat, wine and bread. Three princesses clang their sistra. The Royal Scribe and Steward Apy calls Nefertiti "the hereditary princess, great in favor, lady of grace, dowered with gladness; the Aten rises to shed favor on her and sets to multiply her love; the great and beloved wife of the king, Mistress of South and North, Lady of the Two Lands, Nefertiti, who lives always and for ever."

"The hereditary princess, great of favor, lady of grace, charming in loving-kindness, filling the palace with her beauty, Mistress of South and North, the great wife of the King, whom he loves, the Lady of the Two Lands, who makes the two lands bright with her beauty, the Queen-mother,and great Queen Tiye, mistress of provisions, abundant in fat things. May they abound for the *ka* in a happy life, as provided with pleasure and delight every day."
—*Superintendent Huya*

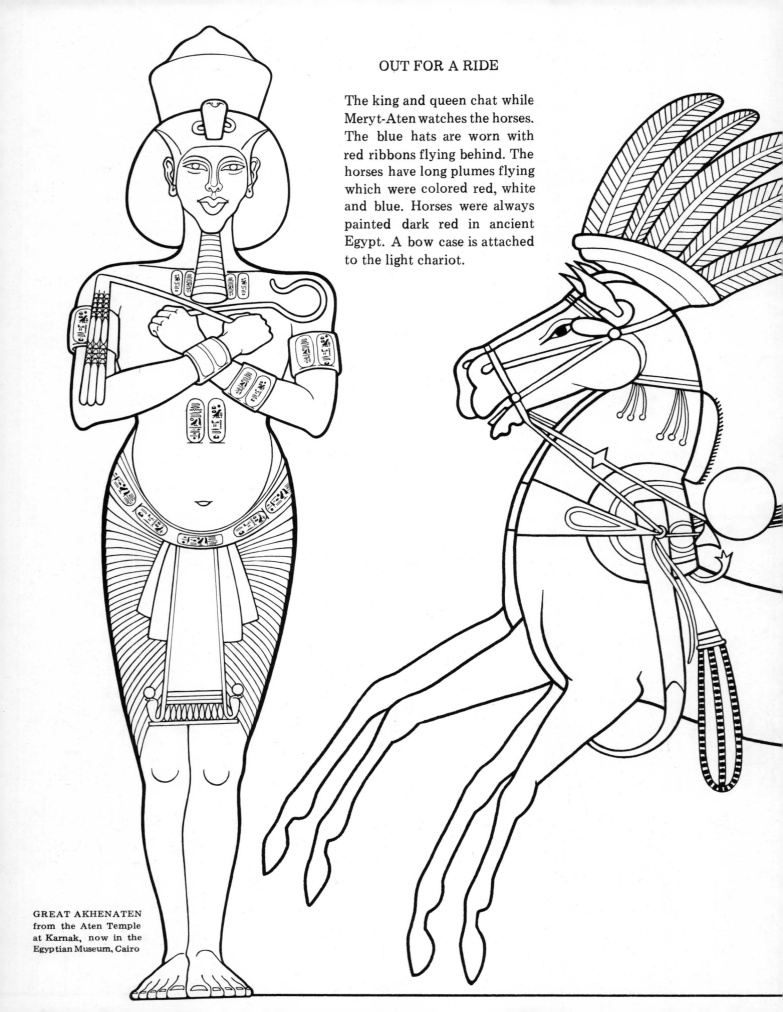

OUT FOR A RIDE

The king and queen chat while Meryt-Aten watches the horses. The blue hats are worn with red ribbons flying behind. The horses have long plumes flying which were colored red, white and blue. Horses were always painted dark red in ancient Egypt. A bow case is attached to the light chariot.

GREAT AKHENATEN
from the Aten Temple
at Karnak, now in the
Egyptian Museum, Cairo

From the tomb of Ahmes

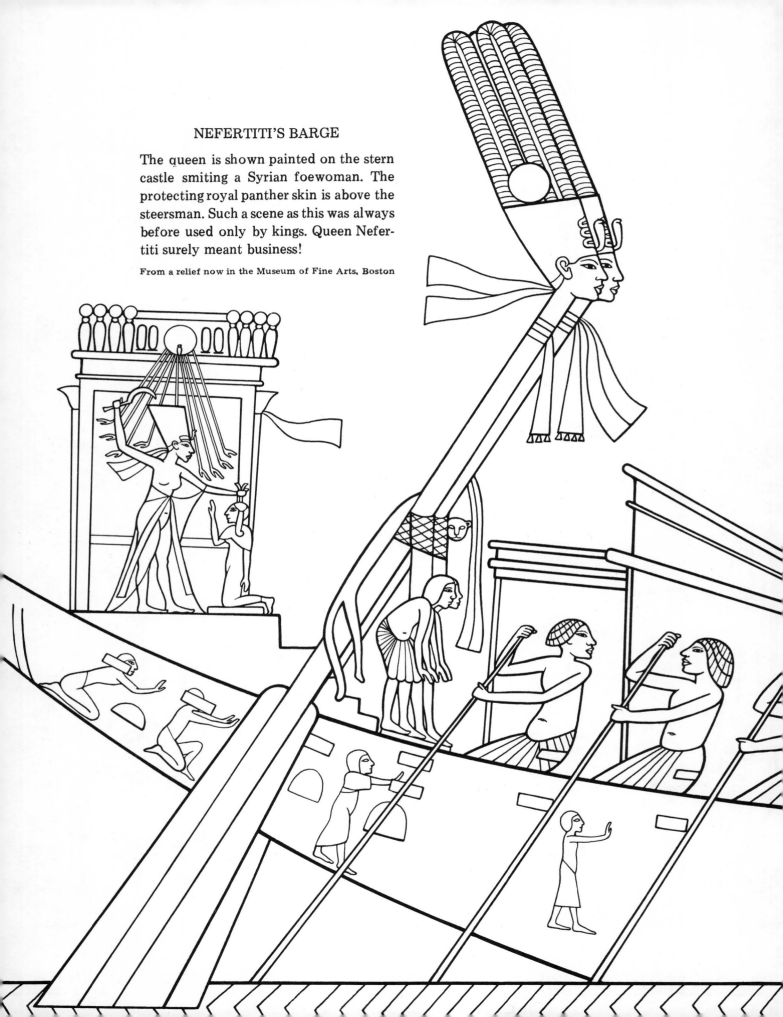

NEFERTITI'S BARGE

The queen is shown painted on the stern
castle smiting a Syrian foewoman. The
protecting royal panther skin is above the
steersman. Such a scene as this was always
before used only by kings. Queen Nefertiti surely meant business!

From a relief now in the Museum of Fine Arts, Boston

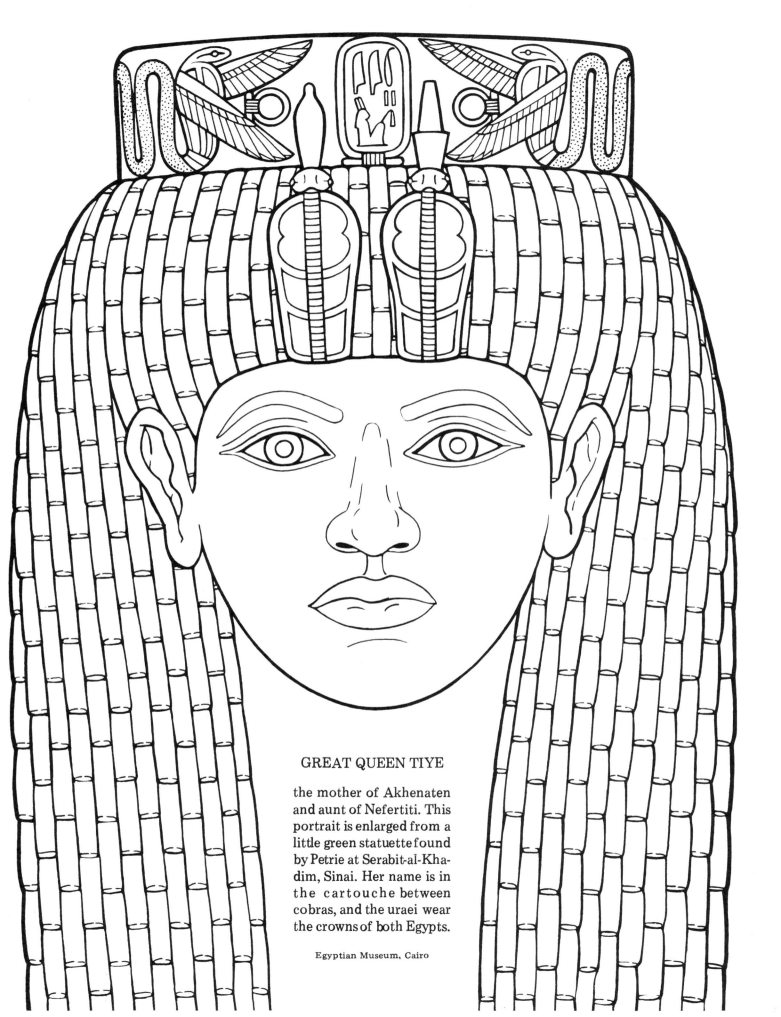

GREAT QUEEN TIYE

the mother of Akhenaten
and aunt of Nefertiti. This
portrait is enlarged from a
little green statuette found
by Petrie at Serabit-al-Kha-
dim, Sinai. Her name is in
the cartouche between
cobras, and the uraei wear
the crowns of both Egypts.

Egyptian Museum, Cairo

Nefertiti is usually shown on equal terms with Akhenaten in ceremonies of offering at altars, purifying, anointing, dining, etc., but here Queen Tuya sits in the honored spot, with her own daughter Beket-Aten beside her. Both queens were advisors to Akhenaten. Nefertiti disappeared in Akhenaten's 12th year and probably died then. Her daughter Meryt-Aten took over as heiress, and soon married Smenkhkare, Akhenaten's younger brother who became co-ruler for a short time. Meryt-Aten died; Smenkhkare then married Ankhes-en-Aten, her younger sister; then Smenkhkare died. Young Tut-ankh-Aten married Ankhes-en-Aten. Tut-ankh-Aten/

Amun, after his short reign, was followed by Ay, Nefertiti's father, who also had a short reign, and who was followed by Horemhab, who married Mut-nodjme, thought to have been Nefertiti's sister. Horemhab destroyed Akhenaten's monuments and removed his name everywhere he could, to make it seem as though Akhenaten had never ruled at all, that Horemhab had succeeded Amenophis III.

From the tomb of Huya

"Nefertiti, living with thee for ever, the great royal wife, his beloved one, Lady of the Two Lands, Nefertiti being at his side, while he gives satisfaction to thy heart and seeth what thou hast made each day. He rejoices at seeing thy beams." —Mery-Re, *High Priest of the Aten*

Above the pool are the dom-palm, the date palm and plane trees. On the right are pomegranate trees. The trees were banked so the roots might be flooded with water from the pool, for the garden depended upon good irrigation.

THE ROYAL GARDEN

From the tomb of Mery-Re

Akhenaten reigned for seventeen years and then was followed by his younger brother, Tut-ankh-Aten, who was nine years old at the start of his sole reign and reigned only one or two years. Tut-ankh-Aten married Ankhes-en-pa-Aten, third daughter of Nefertiti and, probably, Akhenaten, for the succession went through the female line. Tut-ankh-*Amun* (his name changed) and Egypt soon returned to the old gods, for the land had not done well with Akhenaten's new religion.